Riding Sideways

MY JOURNEY WITH ALS

Darla Burns

ISBN-10: 1477603166
EAN-13: 9781477603161

Special thanks to my General Editor,

Wes Burns

Introduction

I have been living with ALS (Amyotrophic Lateral Sclerosis / aka Lou Gehrig's Disease) for six years. The neurologist that diagnosed me told me that my case was atypical because it was progressing slowly. She said that the average time between diagnosis and death is one to three years. The only references I had for people with ALS were: Lou Gehrig (The Pride of The Yankees, 1942, black and white, Gary Cooper movie), the genius, theoretical physicist Stephen Hawking, Morrie Schwartz (from Mitch Albom's book - Tuesdays With Morrie) and Rob Borsellino (columnist for the Des Moines Register). He was a terrific read and, sadly, was taken from this world in May 2006 - just two months after the onset of my symptoms.

Nowadays when people battle illnesses they often blog about it or use their Facebook page. I had no interest in 'journaling' my experiences for myself, let alone anyone else. In fact, I tried to keep it as private as possible for as long as possible. So, why did I want to write a book? I guess I had never seen a book written by a 'regular person' living with ALS. I get that. Many people would, quite literally, run out of time or they would have more urgent priorities. Some of you might think I wanted a way to vent and something to busy myself with. You might be partly right. However, I found other reasons more compelling.

Although I had spent my entire adult life working in the field of disability, I found myself continuously being surprised by the actions of people in general. I found myself saying, "I could write a book." How many people have uttered that phrase? The more important reason for me: I miss words! Not just being able to speak but the fluidity of speech, the reciprocity of conversation, being able to use the nuances of language, to turn a phrase.

I also miss the feeling of my hands on a keyboard and the speed at which my thoughts could spill out through my fingertips. Do not misunderstand. I am extremely grateful for this device I am using to write and communicate. It really is amazing technology that allows me to do multiple things with only my eyes. But, Stephen Hawking I am not.

The final impetus to write was when I met Keith Miner. He is twenty-eight years old, has a lovely wife and a beautiful little boy and Keith has ALS. He didn't just deal with his own 'stuff' - he committed himself to helping others. Keith loves racing so he formed a nonprofit that allows him to use racing to raise money to give financial assistance to families burdened by ALS. What a guy! I realized if he can do that then I can certainly write.

After the initial shock wore off I had to decide how I would deal with ALS. With this kind of thing staring you in the face you quickly learn what you're made of. It came down to what made me . . . me. The sum total of my life experiences, the family I grew up in and my faith.

My mom had a big influence on my life view but maybe not in the way you might think. My mother has not been on this planet for a couple of decades but she is forever in my heart and mind. She would have, and did, whatever was in her power to help her children. She left me with a number of wonderful gifts. She taught me to love learning and literature. She gave me an appreciation for cooking and preparing beautiful food. She showed me what it was to treasure family and how traditions and making memories are at the heart of that. She demonstrated an ability to continuously make something from nothing. Although not a religious woman, she was a woman of faith and shared that as well. She was awesome but, as we all are, she was not without flaws. She had been through her own share of challenges that had deeply affected her. These experiences had taught her to expect the worst out of situations. Her words and responses to those situations have echoed in my head. However, they made me want to be the opposite.

I decided I was not going to let my future with ALS destroy my present. My mantra for my journey would be: plan for the future but live for today, be thankful for something every day, and keep my sense of humor.

That brings us to Riding Sideways. As I began this journey I quickly realized that there would be concessions along the way that would make life easier for me or my husband. This notion is most simply represented by the way we traveled back and forth to work. We have a side loading van with the front passenger seat removed. Now, I can maneuver my chair into position to be locked down beside the driver for travel. However, we found it significantly quicker to lock my chair down facing the side entrance. This concession is representative of all the others that were to come. When you ride sideways in life you see things differently. This is my account of what I have seen.

CHAPTER 1

The Diagnosis

It is surreal how some moments in time are so ordinary when you are experiencing them and yet when you look back they became 'frozen in time' moments. It was summer of 2006. Life was good! My daughter, Charity, was visiting. We were in the car in the garage getting ready to go shopping. I was struggling to start the car. I casually mentioned that I had noticed recently that in order to turn the key in the ignition I had to grasp it with my whole hand. Charity said, "Mom, you were having trouble starting the car last time I was home [several months ago]. You should get that checked out." I have never been one to rush to see a doctor, ever. So, per my usual, I waited. Other than loss of strength I was unaware of anything else. Then I started to look at my hand. With close inspection I could see that the muscle between my thumb and index finger was softer. I also found that the muscle on the 'meatier' part of my palm was softer as well. These were such slight differences that no one would ever notice. I am not sure I would have noticed if it had been in my non-dominant hand. Still, I did not make an appointment with my doctor. It didn't hurt. Wait a minute. It didn't hurt? I had no medical training whatsoever, but even I started to suspect that this thing might not be a simple fix. I made an appointment. My physician, Dr. Terrill, looked at my hand and I think he knew in that moment what I was in for. He wanted me to see a neurologist the next week. He said it could be a brain tumor. I told him it would have to wait because we were going to Florida to visit our daughter and her husband.

When we returned it was the second week of October and the appointments and tests began. The first appointment was with the neurologist. The second visit was for a test at the hospital next door to his office building. The third visit was back to the neurologist for results. The fourth visit was back to the hospital for another test. Our home is in Marshalltown and the neurologist's office is, thankfully, only thirty minutes away in Ames. For scheduling purposes there were always a few days in between appointments. The appointments were full of vagueness and comments about "ruling out" this or that and the need for "tertiary" care. I was getting a little concerned. I had never heard that word before.

The time for appointment number five, my last local appointment, was approaching. So, I did what any confused and uninformed patient does . . . I went to the internet. Of course the first rule of online medical research is to use a reputable source. So, long before I physically went to the Mayo Clinic, I went to their website. I was alone in the house. I brought the laptop into the living room and sat down on the couch. I was about to have another one of those 'frozen in time' moments again. "ALS . . . weakness, often beginning in one body part, often a hand or foot, and loss of muscle tissue or atrophy . . ." As I read the words on the screen a feeling came over me that I had never felt before. It was a sinking feeling that I felt deep, deep in my gut. I had heard that phrase before and thought that I knew what it meant. I did not. I experienced such a heaviness that felt as though I was becoming one with the couch. I am sure that, had I been standing, I would have fainted. Even though I was alone I remember covering my mouth with both hands and leaning forward toward the screen. It was too much to take in.

I immediately began the internal dialogue of, No way! That's impossible. It has to be something else. Fast forward a couple of days. One last appointment and then they planned to refer me to Mayo Clinic. My husband, Ed, was very busy at work so we decided that I would go alone. I planned to work that morning and be home before he came home from work. Now I can hear some of you thinking. "Are you serious? What do you mean he isn't going with?" Stop right there. While I consciously worked at being a positive person, for Ed it was completely natural. Call it denial. Call it ignorance. Call it faith. I had convinced myself, at least 95% of the way, this was going to be something else. Ed's sister, Sharon, called. Although she lived a short distance away we had never been terribly close. There were no bad feelings between us. We had just lived parallel lives, seeing each other at holidays. I told her about my appointment. Knowing my independent nature and, perhaps, reading between the lines much more than I did she simply said, "Why don't I just take you." It really was more of a statement than a question. I didn't really put up a lot of argument. It was a gorgeous fall day. I worked that morning, as planned. I got into her car and as she backed out of the driveway I told her about my plan. I said, "I am not getting a hint of a diagnosis. Today the neurologist I have been seeing is at a conference so I will be seeing a doctor I have never met. I want to be somewhat prepared when I go to Mayo so I did some looking on line. I know I'm being ridiculous but I have to ask if my symptoms are consistent with ALS." We found other topics of conversation and avoided the elephant in the car for the rest of the trip.

The appointment consisted of more results that showed nothing. So, I calmly asked my question. "Are my symptoms consistent with ALS?" The answer did not fit any possible script in my head. A very somber look came across his face. He said, "Why? Did the doctor tell you that last week?" Then, instead of maintaining eye contact with me, his eyes started to dart back and forth between my sister-in-law and me. The tears began to stream down my face as I shook my head no. Sharon explained about the Mayo website. Then he said it. "Yes. We have ruled out a cervical or brain tumor so a neuromuscular disease, most likely ALS, is probable." He kept talking for a bit. It sounded distant and fragmented. He said something about more tests and not being completely sure yet. Oh yes, and we could feel free to use the room as long as we liked. We hugged and cried and time stood still. I still am not sure how long we were in there.

As we walked back to the car it occurred to me that I had never envisioned a circumstance where a brain tumor would have been good news. If there was one thing I had already learned was that ALS had no cure, no treatment. In no way do I mean to make light of brain tumors. In fact, since that day I have known two wonderful women who were diagnosed, fought the good fight, and have already moved on. Every disease has its' own set of struggles and, unfortunately, there is more than enough pain to go around.

As we started to make our way toward home I realized that Sharon taking me to my appointment was a 'God thing'. She was the perfect person to have with me. I know she loves me but not too much. I'm not sure if Ed or one of my sisters would have been really safe driving home. On top of that she took charge and stopped at Dr. Terrill's office on the way home. Sharon knew I would need some medication to help me sleep later. While we waited I remember asking her to promise me that when I ended up in a nursing home she would come put my earrings in and forbid them to dress me in sweat pants. Tears just kept falling. I couldn't stop them.

We were able to see Dr. Terrill and he assured me that, whatever the case, he would go through this with me, and he has.

Dr. Terrill and I had not always been on such good terms. To say that our relationship had been contentious would be a huge understatement. Let me just say that he was not known for his tact or having a gentle bedside manner. Over the course of twenty-five years of care I learned that when the going gets tough you want him on your side. He cared for my children as they were growing up, even though his office did not ac-cept children as patients. My father had a laundry list of health problems and Dr. Terrill managed all of them and added quality and years to Dad's life. Dr. Terrill moved out of the community for a while and I was so unhappy with the other doctors that I just quit going. I have changed and he has mellowed. When was the last time you heard of a doctor being 100% accessible to a patient? He gave us every possible phone number so that we could call any time, day or night. I would like to think that he felt he could do that because we would not use them unless re-ally necessary. He has even made house calls. I didn't think any doctor did that these days. I can't really make you understand how vital Dr. Terrill's care and accessibility have contributed to my sanity and positive attitude. I am just so thankful that I don't have to go through this without him.

I must tell you that when you go to Mayo you bring your diagnostic records with you. I read the records and my suspicions were right. Both Dr. Terrill and the neurologist knew the first time they looked at my hand that I most likely had ALS. That really made me wonder what the plan had been. Were they going to send me to Mayo with no clue? I was so thankful that I had asked. If I hadn't asked I cannot imagine that the visit to Mayo would have been very beneficial. I couldn't imagine that I would have been able to take in much of what they had to say.

What little I knew about ALS I already felt as if I had been hit by a truck and I was being drug by it. What I didn't know was how long it would drag me and how rough the terrain would be.

CHAPTER 2

Mayo

Thanks to Dr. Terrill being proactive and unwilling to take no for an answer I didn't have to wait long for an appointment. I don't know who he knew there or what strings he pulled but he got me in really quickly.

For those of you who have never been, the clinic is a very impressive place. If there is a specialty for a medical problem it can surely be found at Mayo Clinic. I won't bore you with the tedious details of the appointments and tests but I would like to share some of the highlights of my experiences.

The first time we entered the clinic from the parking structure the architecture and overall design were not lost on me. The elevator doors opened and before us was an expansive incline that seemed to bid you to walk up into the light. It was as if you could sense the hope of thousands of people who came, day after day, knowing that if there was hope to be found, it would be here.

As patients go through their itinerary of appointments for a variety of tests, technicians and physicians they end up in countless waiting rooms. I began to make my way through my itinerary and got a glimpse of just how large and valuable the clinic really is. Scanning the waiting rooms I saw teenagers, parents, young adults, couples, and grandparents from all over the world. Some were travelling light while others appeared to be in for the long haul. They had bags stuffed with creature comforts and distractions: drinks, snacks, magazines, books, knitting, notebook computers, handheld games, extra sweaters, blankets and pillows. The emotions in the rooms were palpable.

All these years later I can still see one young couple. They had to be in their twenties, too young for whatever their heavy, heavy burden was. She was in a wheelchair, but not her own, probably a loaner available at the entrance. The chair did not fit her and she looked foreign to it. They had parked the chair at the entrance to the room but turned away from the room so it was facing the hallway. She was thin and had lovely long hair. She sat slumped against one side with her head resting on one hand while her other hand was draped on the arm of the chair. Her husband knelt on the floor facing her with his hand on top of hers. They did not speak. Their position made me wonder, could she not bear to look at the waiting room full of others in similar situations? Did she not want others to see her pain? Was this her first time at the clinic? They had none of the distractions with them to indicate that they had given any thought to the process, only the appointment. They were casually and simply dressed and were representative of the middle class people who seemed to be in the majority in the waiting areas.

Mayo is also known as the destination for the wealthy, celebrities and world leaders. Ed and I happened to be at Mayo on June 18, 2008. We were across the street sitting outside so I could enjoy a Starbucks latte rather than 'hospital coffee'. A series of black SUVs with darkened windows came rushing around the corner right in front of us. They all quickly parked one behind the other, just down the block in front of the Kahler Grand Hotel. Men in black suits, with not so mysterious bulges, jumped out and stood shoulder to shoulder facing each other making a hallway of sorts. Four men split into pairs, walking away from the rows of men in opposite directions. They walked briskly, eyes quickly scanning back and forth and disappeared around their respective corners. You could not see the dignitary being protected as he and all of his guards followed each other into the hotel. It was all over just as quickly as it started. The news later reported that dignitary was Jalal Talibani, the first freely elected president of Iraq. They reported that he was there for knee surgery. Much later it was learned that, in truth, he was there for heart surgery. For obvious reasons they were hiding that fact. Someone told us that there is an underground tunnel connecting the hotel to the clinic. I have no idea if that is true but it certainly seems plausible.

No matter what your status in life, if you think your troubles are big you don't have to look far to find someone with bigger ones. Believe it or not that even applies to ALS. I have read stories about and met parents with ALS who have very young children. As much as I was hurting I was thankful that my children were grown.

My understanding is that in order to meet the criteria for the ALS diagnosis the symptoms must be present in three parts of your body. In addition, the symptoms must be twofold. There is activity in the muscle when the muscle is at rest and muscle wasting or atrophy. Regardless of how much it seems you have ALS you don't have it until the tests prove that you do.

You know you are facing a terrible disease when doctors at one of the most prestigious medical facilities in the country tell you they are hopeful that they will find a different diagnosis. After some very long stressful days full of tests the conclusion was, although I didn't yet meet the criteria, there wasn't anything else it could be. Being in the early stage of the disease was both a curse and a blessing. It was all overwhelming but some comments from my neurologist resonated with me. "This was in your DNA. There was nothing you did to cause it and nothing you can do to make it go away." Oh yes, I also got the "Go home and put your affairs in order, try not to dwell on it and be happy." I am not kidding, they really said that. So I knew but I didn't know. The plan? Return in six months to repeat some of the tests.

The large waiting area at the entrance is flanked on one side by offices etcetera and on the other by a myriad of hallways and elevators leading patients and families toward their particular specialist's offices. It has a two story ceiling. At one end of the space there is a permanent fixture that is well known to anyone who has visited the clinic, a beautiful grand piano. There are probably a million stories about that piano. This is my favorite because it is mine.

During one visit we were sitting and waiting in between appointments and had tired of reading and small talk. All we felt was a great heaviness and out of nowhere came this voice that sounded like it should have been on Broadway. I truly thought we were hearing a recording. Then I realized that people from every part of this great hall were on their feet and moving in the direction of the piano. I sensed movement on the upper level and I looked up to find the railing lined with people who worked at the clinic as well as patients and families. We learned later that musicians often stop at the piano and play and or sing with accompaniment. This man's voice made the hair on the back of your neck stand up. Clearly this man was special. I will never know what his story was but his performance touched me and hundreds of others that day. The song: "To Dream the Impossible Dream".

CHAPTER 3

Grief And Faith

I had become a Christian at age thirteen. Although my family was not part of a church I was. This church warmly welcomed me as part of their family. I was involved in activities and service opportunities. It was a rich learning environment and, as a result, I ultimately attended Central Bible College which trained people for the ministry. I obtained a Bachelor of Arts degree in Christian Education but I primarily went there to study sign language. In addition to course work they also had a program for deaf students. Consequently, I had two deaf roommates and many deaf friends.

Flash forward a few decades and my husband and I had found a different church to call home. Our new church had many lovely and dedicated members. For no particular reason we had not involved ourselves in activities but we felt at home there. In between trips to Mayo we were at church service, sitting in the back row. My emotions were so raw at this time that I quietly cried through the entire service. When the service was over a couple that we had known for almost thirty years, Mike and Cheryl, and another man from the congregation came and sat down on either side of us. We filled them in regarding what was happening. I think we all thought that, sooner or later, the pastor would come back and join us in the now empty room. He did not. One of the men went to find him and brought him back. We prayed together and then went our separate ways.

After the last appointment at Mayo we started the 4 hour drive home. Tears fell silently on and off all the way home. It was dark and there was not much conversation. The next day we both went to work. I don't know what I was thinking. I couldn't keep it together. I came home and returned to the couch, the same spot where I had diagnosed myself on the website. I felt so alone. Everyone I knew was at work. I wanted, more than anything, to be close to my husband. Grief will make you do funny things. It sounds silly but I got his pajamas and held them close. They had his scent and it helped comfort me.

I began to talk to God. I suppose it was praying but not like I had done before. At that point all I could say was, "HELP". I did something I had never done in my life. I picked up the phone and called 'our' church for help. I did not receive the response I expected. Instead, I was told that the pastor was in a meeting and then would be leaving for lunch. Was my voice not desperate enough? Did I not make it clear that I was a little afraid of being alone? If learning that you have a terminal illness, especially one like ALS, is not cause for help what is? I got a return phone call a couple of hours later and a prayer over the phone. I felt wounded. Having graduated from a Bible college

I knew about ministry so it wasn't like I expected the pastor to rush over. Also, having worked in the field of helping people, I am confident that, at the very least, I would have inquired if this was something urgent or if there was someone else who could help me. I guess I did expect to receive a follow up call or visit from someone.

It would not be that way for long. Phone calls, cards, flowers and emails started to come in from near and far. Churches in Iowa, Arizona and Florida were praying for me. I genuinely felt the prayers holding me up.

A lady I didn't know from a church I had never been to, sent me a prayer shawl. If you don't know what that is, let me explain. It was made by women of faith and as they were knitting or crocheting they were praying for the recipient. I considered it an honor to receive one. Mine was a lovely shade of green and it was long enough to wrap around me. When my emotions are in turmoil I feel cold on the inside. I wrapped up in my shawl frequently. As the ALS progressed I found that I was often literally cold. I still feel blessed every time I use it.

Mike and Cheryl kept in regular contact by phone. One day they called to invite us to a healing prayer service in a nearby town. It was a nondenominational church without a congregation, known as the House of Prayer. To most of you this probably strikes you as one of the stages of grief - bargaining. To the rest of you it may seem desperate or just weird. I didn't think it was either one of those things. I was touched by their thoughtfulness. The Bible teaches that God heals. I believe that He continues to heal people today. I also believe in divine guidance and healing through medicine. I also know that godly people die every day. God does what He does for His purposes. When physical healing does not occur God has another purpose. It may be spiritual healing of the individual, a family, a community or even a church. Ultimately aren't we all healed when we go home to be with Him in heaven? That being said, I plan to be at 'the head of the line', so to speak, to ask for some clarification about that. Clearly I was not physically healed but I felt God's strength and love through those who became avenues of His power that evening. God is the author of peace, and I felt that peace.

Just because I have faith doesn't mean I was always strong. I had many moments of weakness, and still do.

CHAPTER 4

Now What?

I always hear people say, "I know what I would do if. . ." No, you don't. Without variation I had always been a person who processed challenges, medical or otherwise, cerebrally. I would research through whatever means possible and leave no stone unturned. Not this time. I had read briefly about the end game that first glance at the Mayo website. I had been given a clear picture at my appointments at Mayo. I knew if I stared into the abyss I would go downhill quickly, at least mentally.

I decided - no pity parties, and it worked...most of the time. Instead of saying, "Why me?" my life experiences had taught me to say, "Why not me?" There is all manner of suffering in the world and, unless you are going through life with your eyes closed, you don't have to work to find it. I knew a young couple whose first child was born with cancer. How could I possibly compare to that?

Life went forward pretty much the same. My fight was spiritual and mental, not medical. As I said in the introduction my goal became to plan for the future but live for today, be thankful for something every day and to keep my sense of humor.

Planning for the future was about both the immediate and the long range future. For the immediate future I knew that it was vital to keep working. It was really great medicine. I loved my job! Not to mention we needed the income. (ALS can be very expensive.) I wanted to work as long as possible.

The initial work modifications were small: pens with adaptive grips, a new office chair that was taller so that it was easier to rise from, both a manual and an electric seat assist (portable devices that kind of push you up to help you stand) and a signature stamp. I also took two of my favorite scriptures and taped them to the parameter of my computer screen.

> ***Philippians, chapter 4 - verses 7 and 8*** *"And the peace of God, which passeth all understanding, shall keep your hearts and minds through Christ Jesus. Finally, brethren, whatsoever things are true, whatsoever things are honest, whatsoever things are just, whatsoever things are pure, whatsoever things are lovely, whatsoever things are of good report; if there be any virtue, and if there be any praise, think on these things."*

> ***1 Corinthians, chapter 14, verse 33*** *"For God is not the author of confusion, but of peace, as in all churches of the saints."*

Things continued to change and I continued to adapt. I altered the way I used the computer keyboard and my speed slowed down a bit.

At home the early adaptions were small as well. They included: a used recliner with a power lift, a potato peeler that hooked on my finger and fit in the palm of my hand and a self-opening can opener.

I needed help to know what to do next both at work and at home. The help I needed was available from Vocational Rehabilitation. In order to apply I would need documentation of my disability, the definitive diagnosis.

I had cancelled the six month return appointment at Mayo but now it was time to go back. We made that return appointment. Some of the tests were repeated and the diagnosis criteria were met quickly. The clinic, just as other hospitals, offer special clinic dates where the patient stays put while any number of specialists come to the patient. I opted out of that follow up as well. Perhaps I saw this differently than most but I did not want to measure my losses. I didn't want to know what to expect to lose next. It may have been foolishness but I thought if I didn't expect it then I would avoid the self-fulfilling prophecy.

In October 2008 I became a client of Vocational Rehabilitation. I preferred 'client' to 'patient'. At least as a client there was something to do. I found the 'nothing to be done' aspect of ALS difficult. It was hard to overhear people ask friends battling cancer for updates. Over and over people inquired about how they were feeling and when they would be done with treatment. I certainly did not begrudge them this kindness. I did not desire the attention. I was jealous that they had something to do and a hope for a better outcome.

Now I had something to do. As a Vocational Rehabilitation client I was assigned a counselor to help me obtain the right assessments and, subsequently, the appropriate equipment. There was financial assistance based on our income but of equal, or perhaps more, value was my counselor, Barb. She shared my positive outlook and used her skills and expertise to develop a plan to help me achieve my immediate goal. She made an appointment at the University of Iowa for assessing what some of my needs were and joined us for the appointment. I had good energy but my legs were becoming weaker and I had fallen several times. I was definitely going to need a power wheelchair. So, while we were there I sat in a power wheelchair. Barb, Ed and I were in a hallway and I drove the chair down the hallway, facing away from them. Since it was late fall the first thought in my head was, 'Great! I can go Christmas shopping.' Then I turned around and saw the look in Ed's eyes. We almost lost it but Barb reminded us that a few minutes earlier we had commented that our stubbornness would be our combined strength. In November 2008 I was measured and 'fit' for a power wheelchair. Due to a long arduous battle with the insurance company and the durable medical equipment vender I kept waiting and falling. I finally got my chair on St. Patrick's Day 2009.

With Barb's help we found a used van with a drop down side ramp and a used lift to install in the garage so that I could get into my home. The weird thing is when you are able to obtain used equipment it is probably because one of two things has happened. Either the previous owner's disease has progressed to the point that they are no longer able to use it or they have moved on to the next world. This was our experience in obtaining equipment but I fully expect that will also be the case when I'm gone and that comforts me.

We had to remodel our home to accommodate my wheelchair and my needs in the restroom. Vocational Rehabilitation rules allow assistance only for those things needed to prepare for work (the bathroom), and to get in and out of the house. This is how it should be as they are being good stewards of public funds. The plans for each person are individualized. To put it simply, nothing extra is done. So, for our home that meant the rear entrance to the house. This meant enlarging the door and building a platform so that I could drive my chair off of the lift and into the house. Other changes included my bedroom door and the bathroom. There are parts of my home I cannot access but because of my limitations there is no need for me to do so.

Since my voice was strong I was able to use a voice recognition software program that afforded me full access on the computer. My desk was raised to accommodate my wheelchair. Those were probably the "easy fixes". The more challenging accommodations were extra hands whenever I needed them. My boss, Rich, went over and above what anyone would consider fair or reasonable. There was always someone to arrange my paperwork on my desk, retrieve files for me or assist me with the phone. Towards the end of my work he encouraged me to work from home when possible. My colleagues were amazing and I could not have done it without them.

As for the long range planning there were things to do to get my house in order, both figuratively and literally. We bought our final piece of real estate, two plots near my parents. Along with that we selected, purchased and had our 'marker' installed. Due to the circumstances we were able to access some retirement funds to improve our finances a bit, in anticipation of reduced income. After thirty years of marriage, like most couples, we each had our roles around the house. I needed to transfer my responsibilities to my husband. It is not as easy as it sounds, from either side of the fence. The most difficult for me was to hand over my kitchen. I loved to cook and bake. I knew I had succeeded when he went out one day and came back with the most masculine looking hand mixer I had ever seen. The most difficult thing for him to assume was the bill paying and record keeping. Everyone has their own system and it was a challenge to take over my system and make it into a system that works for him.

There was 'housekeeping' to take care of while I was still able to do it with help. I had a large collection of cookbooks, many of which rarely got used. Two former colleagues were pleased to take them off my hands.

I had accumulated a fair bit of craft supplies over the years and I was really into scrapbooking. Charity had done some scrapbooking so she took a few things. Some items could be used in children's crafts so they were passed on to a dear woman who volunteered with a church sponsored after school program.

There were closets of clothing that did not work well for my limited flexibility or being in the wheelchair. Then, there were the shoes. My collection was not extensive or expensive but I loved them. Some of these were given to my sister and the rest to Goodwill.

Was I sad about giving these things away? I would be lying if I said "no". Did I sit and cry about it? Not really. It felt good to pass these things on to people who would enjoy them. It felt even better to accomplish something that would lessen the burden on my family in the future. My viewpoint on these tasks was to do them and move on. Of everything I gave away I only think about the shoes, just now and then.

"Live for today" had more meaning than "stop and smell the roses". For me it meant concentrating on what was right in front of me. I wanted to do whatever I could for as long as I could. I cooked for as long as I was able. I can even tell you what I cooked last. I made pancakes from scratch; no pancake mix was ever used in our house. I can also tell you about the last time I hugged my children. I knew that it wouldn't be long before I would no longer be able to hug them. I didn't know it was the final hug but it was. I was heading to bed and I needed help to walk. I could not stand for long. Ed was helping me walk the short distance and I asked him to stop. I leaned against the living room wall, locked my knees and asked them to give me a hug. I can recall it like yesterday. Of course, I still get hugs from people who love me. They are great - but hugs, by their very definition, are meant to be shared.

For almost thirty Christmases I had made a gingerbread creation. They included: a log cabin, a Victorian home, a church with stained glass windows, a covered bridge with a family of ice skaters on the river below, Santa's workshop, Santa's barn - complete with Santa in his sleigh with all of his reindeer harnessed and ready to go, a trio of village stores - including a toy store and a bakery with three tiny gingerbread houses in the front window, and a nativity. December 2008 was the last gingerbread house I made without help. It was a simple cottage but I did it. December 2009 was the final gingerbread house in our home. It was the one I had always wanted to do. It was a replication of my grandmother's farm house, complete with outhouse. The real house had been gone for years so I worked from pictures. I had lots of help but it was a perfect final house. My gingerbread creations had achieved my original intention. I had wanted to create Christmas memories for my children that were not dependent on how much money we did or didn't have but yet were uniquely theirs.

We had good parties with positive, upbeat friends that were great fun! We took a couple of trips but I will tell you more about that later.

"Live for today" also took on an important meaning when dealing with my doctor and other medical professionals. Part of using a power wheelchair is maintaining it and, as the ALS progresses, making sure that it still fits your needs. A group of medical professionals from the University of Iowa Hospital and Clinics travel to communities to assess chairs and make recommendations. The local vender who sold you the chair is also there to implement or procure the modifications and install them. My left hand rested in a "U" shaped handle and I operated my wheelchair by pushing with my arm. At one point the recommendation was for me to switch to a headrest that doubles as a driving mechanism. The chair is operated by 'tapping' either side or the back of the headrest. I wanted to maintain as long as I could and not hurry into the future. Although I knew I would soon have no choice for the time being I chose to delay the change. Dr. Terrill looks toward the future and counsels me about options and plans. I sometimes invoke the "not today" phrase with him as well.

The second part of my mantra was "be thankful for something every day". I had and have a great deal to be thankful for. In the beginning it was very easy. My understanding was that when ALS begins in the extremities you have more time. I used to tell people, "I'm still walking and talking".

When I was still walking I was thankful for every person who helped pick me up after I fell. This was a wide range of people: a stranger in the grocery store, a neighbor, a coworker, a family member or an ambulance attendant.

I was also grateful for all of the people who helped in different ways. One snowy evening we went to see a movie and my husband dropped me off at the entrance, knowing he would be right back to help me with the stairs. I thought I was doing quite well so I started up the stairs on my own. A gentleman appeared at my elbow and said, "Let me help you." It was a statement instead of a question. Then there were times I had to ask for help and, at least once, I think God sent an angel. I was in the ladies room of a nice restaurant and I was stuck. I had already learned the hard way that when you suspect you might have a problem you don't lock the door. That, in and of itself, created problems. This day I was particularly humbled as I was done using 'the facilities' and then I could not stand up. I finally summoned the courage to call out to a lady in the next stall. I asked her to get my husband and then watch the door so no other ladies came in. I couldn't believe what happened next. She said, "No, I'll help" and she came in. She gave me her arm and that was all I needed. I think about her and wonder what led her to be so kind and to go above what many reasonable people would consider acceptable.

Now that I'm no longer walking and barely talking it can be challenging some days, but never impossible.

I am thankful for my brothers Daryl and Cecil, and my two amazing sisters, Barbara and Brenda, who drop everything and come help whenever they are asked. I have the best friend, Sandy. Notice I didn't say 'my' best friend - I said 'the' best friend. Everyone should have a Sandy in their life. She came to see me even when it was really hard for her and laughed and cried with me. Mary Jo, Chris and Maureen keep in touch and visit when they can to keep my spirits up. I have an amazing family and awesome friends.

For about the last two and a half years one real bright spot has been Charity's dog Zoey. She is half Shih Tzu and half Maltese and has the sweetest disposition! When our children were growing up we had a precious little Bichon Frise named Fluffy. Original, right? Actually, it is worse than that. The children were preschoolers when we brought our puppy home and they named her Fluffy Wuffykins. We even registered her that way but it was quickly shortened to Fluffy. When she died she left a big hole in our family and in our hearts. I really miss having a dog but the last thing Ed needs now is something else to take care of. When Charity got Zoey we lovingly referred to her as our 'furry grand baby`. She is so much fun but I find it to be especially sweet how she responds to my wheelchair. A power wheelchair makes a little click sound when you engage the motor and there is a second or two before the chair begins to move. When I leave my bedroom for the first time of the day Zoey hears the click and comes running. She jumps up on my lap, greets me with a lick, turns around and sits down facing forward; as if to say, "Let's go". She stays there just long enough for me to 'drive` to the kitchen. Then she jumps down and runs off to check on other family members. Zoey brings me joy every time she visits.

I could go on and on about things I am thankful for.

The third part of my mantra was to keep my sense of humor. This begins with being positive yourself. Who wants to hang out with someone who is 'doom and gloom'? It will deter people from spending time with you and bring down those who are around you.

I am not saying I was never down. I gave myself permission to have the occasional meltdown. I just try not to stay there. The other part of this that helps me keep my sanity is my belief that the only things that are for now and for always are love and faith. With ALS I am not in charge - it is. This means that I am faced with decisions about an advance directive, or living will, and other questions about 'what if' scenarios. I have a living will and I am sure I will not deviate from it. There are in between decisions and it gives me peace to reserve the possibility that I could change my mind. Some days it would have been easy to give up, stay in bed and let the ALS take over. I am not ready to do that. Not today.

For quite a while I would not watch sad movies. I made a conscious effort to laugh every day. As for my particular sense of humor I'll give you three examples.

When you have ALS and you fall you cannot catch yourself so you fall, literally, flat on your face - arms at your sides. I did that at work. I also landed with my head and shoulders in a doorway. To add to the situation I am not a small woman. It must have really been quite a site. My hair had fallen to cover both sides of my face. I don't know about other people with ALS but for me it helps if you know how to roll me over. So, I heard people around me but I could not lift my head and I was bleeding. I talked them through what to do. They did a great job and I was not seriously injured. The next work day I brought a cake with the message, "THANKS FOR THE HELPING HANDS". On the perimeter of the cake I had the decorator draw a series of hands. In the center of the cake I put a 'Barbie type' doll - face down. I thought it was hysterical. I wanted to genuinely say thanks and to give them permission to laugh.

Shortly after I came home from Mayo a friend basically asked, "Well? What did they tell you?" My response was, "They said I could buy milk and eggs but no three year magazine subscriptions." My family always had an affinity for dark humor.

Sherry is a friend with a similar sense of humor. We were talking one day about how hard it is to stay hydrated when you can't reach a glass or a straw. She offered to make a special hat for me. It would resemble a beer hat with a straw that would be bent to my mouth. Sherry planned to add thick blond yarn braids, just for a little extra fun.

I am not 100% successful every day but I believe I am better for trying.

CHAPTER 5

Traveling With ALS

I've heard it explained that when you have ALS, or another life altering disease, that it is like having a third person in a marriage or traveling with extra baggage, and I am not referring to medical equipment. We certainly learned a great deal, not the least of which is that handicapped accessible has an extremely wide range of meaning.

We had traveled very little in our marriage so we decided to take a trip before I was restricted by my wheelchair. We planned ahead and checked with the airline as to what to do. At this time my biggest concern was being able to stand up when the flight ended. I had to be seated on the aisle with a removable armrest. I needed to be able to turn my legs into the aisle so that I could lean forward in order to stand. The airline representative told us that several of the seats on each plane had removable armrests. They told us it would be accommodated very easily. All I had to do was to identify myself and explain to the airline staff prior to boarding. Now think about it. You could not discern that I had a disability by looking at me. I approached the airline staff prior to boarding and there were no other passengers around. She looked up from the podium and looked from my head to my toes. She angrily proclaimed, "I have no idea if any of the armrests come off. You'll have to speak to a flight attendant on board. I don't have time for this." With that she returned to shuffling her paperwork. Now I had a choice. The old me would have blown my top and asked for her supervisor, at the very least. I would have followed up with a nasty letter to the airline. This would take time and energy, both of which had taken on a much greater value these days. In addition it would have a negative impact on our good mood as we started our trip. Fortunately, Ed is mechanically inclined and we learned that, apparently, all armrests are removable. FYI - none of the flight attendants knew that they could be taken off.

On this trip we rented a car and drove the Pacific Coast Highway from San Francisco to Seattle. Wherever we traveled we requested handicap accessible rooms. Because I was still able to walk we didn't have to be very specific, we thought. Most of the rooms actually did work out, with one exception. Oddly enough we found that there was no relationship between the number and quality of the accessibility features and the size of the community or the sophistication of the hotel. The best room was in a small remote community at an older motel. The room had every kind of accommodation you could envision. Even though I did not yet have a power wheelchair I noticed that there was even an outlet by the bed at arm height.

The worst room was near the airport in Seattle. It was a pricey and luxurious hotel. We checked in and went up to the room. The room was beautiful with especially lovely linens. Then we checked out the bathroom. There was one grab bar in the combination tub / shower. Unless you have ever had difficulty standing from a seated position, I'm not sure if you can appreciate what else we saw. I'm not sure but it may have been the world's smallest toilet. There was no way we could stay there. We went down to the front desk to ask if, perhaps, we were given the wrong room. Remember the airline staff? These people seemed to be competing for rudest hotel staff in America. The woman behind the counter was flanked by four other staff members. She told us that all of the handicapped rooms were identical. I asked if they had ever been approached by anyone regarding the ADA guidelines. You would have thought I had hurled a series of personal assaults at her. She seemed to grit her teeth as she advised me, "We have been in this location long before the ADA and we don't have to meet those guidelines!" I know that the hospitality industry can be demanding but was this outright callous behavior the best she could do? I'm sure she didn't think I looked handicapped but that really wasn't the point. I had the same choice again as to what to do. We moved on and spent our energy making phone calls to find a replacement room. In this age of instant social media one would expect businesses to behave more appropriately. Ah, but wait until you read the next one.

Our wedding anniversary was approaching and I was in the hospital for something unrelated to ALS. I was released and doing well at home so my husband, Ed, made plans for a short trip to Des Moines, a city about an hour away. He made a reservation for a handicap accessible room in a nice motel. At this time I was in the power wheelchair but I could still transfer with

Ed's help. Consequently, Ed made the appropriate inquiries as to the specifics in order to assure it met my needs. He went into the office to check in. The desk staff said nothing of note. We drove around to the back and were surprised to learn that there were a number of quaint little duplex cottages. The only problem was that they all appeared to be tucked into a small hill. There were three cement steps up to the building and one more step up into the room. Again, we thought there must have been a mistake or, if we were lucky, there was a rear at level entrance. We circled the building but to no avail. We made our way back to the motel office and went to the front desk. Now, remember we are clearly together and I am sitting there in my power wheelchair. Ed said, "I think there must have been a mistake. The room you put us in will not work for us." I am not kidding you. The clerk looked at us and said, "What is it about the room that won't work for you?" Ed and I looked at each other in disbelief. We said, "The stairs." Without batting an eye he said, "Oh, we had another couple in the room you reserved and they wanted to stay over." I don't know when I had seen Ed so angry. We all know how motels are supposed to handle this kind of thing. Here again was that choice, only this time there would be a much greater cost if we took the path of negative energy. Ed was already really disappointed and I did not want him to feel any worse. If we had chosen to fight, we might not have gotten the desired result and we would have lost a lot of precious time. We still had to find another motel and go to dinner at a reasonable hour. Ed reminded the clerk that he had ordered something for the room. We left with the one dozen yellow roses he had sent to the room and found another room five minutes down the road.

Our daughter and her family live in the Chicago area. At this writing we have made three trips with the power wheelchair.

Trip 1 - She and her husband, David, had purchased their first home. They had shared lovely apartments but this was their first house. What parent doesn't want to celebrate that with their child? I was using the power wheelchair but I could still walk very short distances. I knew with ALS there is no promise of tomorrow so this might be my only opportunity to see the inside of her home for myself. As a bonus, this would be my only opportunity to spend the night. It warmed my heart to be a part of that weekend. I loved her home and it suited her and David perfectly. The reasons I had to seize this opportunity were the age and style of the home and the unknown of how long it would be before I would not be able to walk at all. It was a midcentury brick bungalow; which meant small doorways and higher thresholds. Since I could still walk the only downside this trip was that I fainted after walking into her house. My doctor told me later that it was probably due to a drop in blood pressure related to being dehydrated. When you travel and you have no idea if, when or where you would find a bathroom that would fit your needs you limit what you drink.

Trip 2 - The birth of our first and only grandchild. (You will hear much more about this later.) Clearly I was not going to miss this but it would require planning and grace. First we had to research motels to find one where the bed is not on a pedestal. I could no longer transfer myself from the wheelchair to the bed. That meant we needed a lift. The lift has two legs that have to slide under the bed. We were on the internet and phone for hours trying to find a motel. Most front desk staff had no idea, so we had to wait on hold or wait for them to call back. Finally we found a match and now we had to arrange for equipment. We learned that there was an ALS loan closet operated by the ALS Association in Chicago. This is a great program but we learned it is best to communicate only through email so that they are clear about what you need. They arranged to have a lift and a transport chair delivered to our motel before we were scheduled to arrive. We were incredibly appreciative; however, we found that the learning curve for the different style lift was too much for a short trip. Because we were unfamiliar with the specifics of this particular lift I did not get seated properly, which resulted in me gradually sliding forward. Of course it was quite embarrassing to have Ed try to save me from sliding out of my chair in the middle of a Buffalo Wild Wings on a busy Friday night. We improved with each use but decided to try to bring our own lift in the future. Now you are likely asking yourself, "If we could do that why didn't we do that in the first place?" Our lift is quite large. It will fit in our van but just barely. First I have to get in and locked down. Then the lift goes in behind me. This means that the reverse procedure must happen in order for me to get out. That means that even if we are going into a restaurant the procedure must be repeated. It can be done but it takes time and patience. It is an inconvenience at best. So we thought it was worth a try. Next time we took our own.

We were also unfamiliar with the term 'transport chair'. It turned out to be a manual wheelchair that has the wheels under the seat. This gives you valuable inches when going through narrower doorways in older buildings. The chair was a bit of a life saver but with ALS, depending on the stage of progression, your core, arms, legs, and head all need the very personalized support of your own chair. Without that you fatigue and have discomfort, but totally worth it for this visit. The only other thing we needed was a set of portable ramps to get the wheelchair into the house. Ed made them and they did the job nicely.

Trip 3 - A visit to our granddaughter. Of course we had to make another visit a few months later. The motel we had used when she was born was close to the hospital. We started the process over to find a motel closer to their home. This time we found a lovely motel and, as I mentioned, we brought our lift. I mention it to share one more piece of the story. At the previous motel the staff had put the chair and the lift in our room prior to our arrival. This time Ed had to move our lift into our room, through the lobby, several stories up on the elevator, down the hall to our room. It was interesting how many people were visibly puzzled by this 'contraption'.

I also had the silly idea that we should request a standard wheelchair to prevent the discomfort I felt in the companion chair. This motel staff held the chair at the front desk instead of putting it in the room. Ed went down to get it and returned with a large box. Yes, he had to assemble the chair. It was then that we learned how much wider it was. It would not fit through the doorways in our daughter's home. Another lesson learned.

Even with all of the challenges we face when we travel at least I am still able to travel. There will come a day when I will no longer be able to do so. But, not today.

CHAPTER 6

Weddings, Funerals And Garage Sitting

Most people take for granted their participation in the events of their lives. There is a freedom that comes with the ignorance of barriers faced daily by individuals with mobility issues. You receive invitations to weddings. A friend dies. A family member has a birthday party. Friends invite you to dinner or a movie. You need a haircut. Your plans have more to do with what you want to wear than whether or not you can physically participate. Early on we learned to call ahead to ask about accessibility and people always said, "Oh yes, we are accessible." I don't believe they are trying to misrepresent the situation. They just don't know.

Four Funerals

Funerals one and two - these funerals were both held in funeral homes. One was in our home town and the other in a smaller town a half hour away. Both of these buildings were modern and, therefore, much more accessible.

Funeral three - the church was fairly modern but built for a small congregation in our home town. It was very small and had a narrow center aisle. The only option was for me to park to one side of it. There really weren't any side aisles. The deceased had chosen to be cremated so there was no coffin to be moved. Still, it was awkward but workable.

Funeral four - the church was a 1950's style building in a small rural community. It had a sizable threshold, which was probably not a significant issue to a standard wheelchair. Depending on the person in the chair, it could be rocked back or lifted over by strong helpers. This is not as easy for a power wheelchair. They are extremely heavy. Even when it is empty a power wheelchair can weigh up to 350 pounds. Some power wheelchairs have gears or settings for higher grades. However, when the chair barely fits through the door it can be problematic to do. In this case it worked with a little push and pull from a few strong men. Once inside we were assured they had a reserved area for wheelchairs. It was the back wall of the sanctuary. So I parked my chair where I was directed by the usher. Ed sat alone in the last pew, approximately six feet in front of me. He refused to sit toward the front with his mother, sisters and other family members. He sat alone and I sat alone staring at his back. This felt lousy.

Five Weddings

Wedding one - a medium size wedding in a beautiful old church in a small town. We called ahead and they informed us they had an elevator to take wheelchairs to the sanctuary. It was an unusual set up. The main entry was at street level and that was no problem. Their "elevator" was a lift intended for a manual wheelchair. In order to use the lift you had to rotate a safety bar over your head. A power wheelchair is too tall. We did not want the bride and groom to feel badly on their special day so we stayed. We sat alone on the lower level and listened to the ceremony through a speaker. We did not attend the reception.

Wedding two - a rather large wedding in another beautiful historic church in a large town. We were told that the entrance was on the lower level and they had an elevator, a real elevator. We were hopeful that this time it would work out. It almost did. The entrance - no problem. The elevator - an actual real elevator. It was small but it fit my chair, me and my husband. A plus for a power wheelchair was that we entered on one side and exited through a door on the opposite side. The last pews in the sanctuary were shortened so it was great. Then the ceremony was over and it got interesting. A small boy got into the elevator and pushed all of the buttons. Yes, the elevator froze. They were able to pull the doors apart to get the boy out. It turns out that they had to call an out of state company to get a repairman. I privately started to panic a little on the inside, wondering how on earth we would get out of this one. We were thrilled to learn that, while the company was out of state, the repairman was local. We ended up waiting about an hour for him to arrive. Thank goodness it didn't take him long to do the repair. Everyone associated with the wedding was so concerned and kind, including the groom. When we were finally free we still had an hour drive ahead of us so we skipped the reception.

Wedding three - another rather large wedding in a more modern building in our home town. We had been in this building for many events over the years, before ALS. The sanctuary was at street level but the reception area was on a lower level. We inquired about access and they were pleased to report that they had an elevator. Experience had taught us to not take anything at face value. A couple of days before the wedding we went over to check it out. They did have an "elevator" but not what you envision when you think of an elevator. It looked more like a lift for freight. It reminded me of a dumb waiter in a professional kitchen I had worked in as a young woman. This was a nicer version and painted a very bright white. There was only room for me and my chair and nothing else! Thank goodness it could be operated from the outside. By this time I was unable to lift my hands to push a button. I got in and we tried it only to learn that it would not fit my needs. It was not suited to the weight of a power wheelchair. Ed also went to the lower level to check the elevator exit. Even if it would have worked I would not have been able to get out of the elevator. The exit required a ninety degree turn which would have been impossible due to the tight fit. I'm sure that people in charge of such installations try to ensure the best outcome they can achieve while being good stewards of their financial resources. Most of these types of 'add ons' go through a committee that do research and make recommendations. There are countless resources to use to assist in the decision making process. I would also recommend finding someone in a power wheelchair or someone with a family member in a power wheelchair and ask for their input. At least they would be making a fully informed decision. Since this was in our home town I decided to stay home and have my sister, Brenda, come hang out while Ed attended the wedding and reception.

Wedding four - a large wedding at a beautiful, modern building in our home town. The building entrance and sanctuary were both at street level. Inside the pews were installed so that there was a center aisle and two side aisles with more pews on either side. Due to the tremendous size of the church wedding guests were only seated in the two center sections. There were no cut outs for wheelchairs, as seen in some public buildings. Obviously, one cannot obstruct the center aisle at a wedding. The outer aisles were fine so it was great to be able to witness their vows and celebrate with them. The reception was in a second location and it was at street level. However, the room was so packed with tables and decorations that I could barely get through. I tried to make my way to the perimeter of the room so that my chair would be as least intrusive as possible. The seated guests seemed to be blind to the chair. Ed had to directly ask people to please stand up so we could go through. Maybe it is just me, but I felt like a major inconvenience.

Wedding five - another rather large wedding at the Reiman Gardens, in Ames. Don't let the name deceive you. It was an indoor wedding in December in Iowa. It was a beautiful facility that was perfect for anyone with mobility issues. The bride and groom planned for guests to be seated at round tables for the ceremony and the reception in the same room. It couldn't have been more perfect if I had planned it myself. I was able to park my chair in such a way that it was unobtrusive. It was also great fun because it was a costume wedding and Wes was the officiate.

Family Members and Holidays.

I have two brothers and two sisters and Ed has two sisters. We are also fortunate to have many friends, both in and out of town. There is not one house in our circle that I can go in. Think about all of the birthdays, Easters, Thanksgivings and Christmases that make up the fabric of your extended family life.

At least here in rural Iowa it is not unheard of to host a high school graduation party or the occasional birthday party in a garage. Not many of the people in our circle have garages but for those who do we have found 'garage sitting' as an acceptable alternative in fair weather. We lived in our first home for over twenty-five years. There was no patio, porch, deck or other kind of place to sit or entertaining space. So, when we were shopping for the home we now live in an outside space was a high priority. Consequently, we have an older, modest deck on the rear of our home. Before ALS I loved to sit on the deck and read, have coffee or lunch, entertain friends or just enjoy the weather. Since I have been in my wheelchair I no longer have access to our deck. Now we garage sit at home as well. We have even put up a folding table and had lunch.

Movies

I have always loved movies! Not just the movies but the whole movie going experience. I enjoyed being part of an audience and listening to the reactions of other people. For thirty-two years I thoroughly enjoyed going to the movies with my husband, Ed. It is part of the shared experience to glance at each other when a particular scene struck a chord or to share the popcorn. Even though we have theaters where we live, we would drive an hour to have a different theatre experience or to see an independent film that would not come to our town. Sometimes we would time it right and take in a double feature by quickly driving across town. After ALS and the wheelchair movies are not nearly as enjoyable. When I'm in the chair my head is two feet above his. For some reason I can't conceive of the theater seats are very close to the floor. In order to share popcorn he almost has to stand up. It makes it equally difficult to make eye contact or hold hands. Once in a while we still go to a movie but generally we watch movies through Netflix.

Hair

I found the loss of the ability to do my hair, apply make-up and put in my earrings especially difficult. My husband does everything for me but he drew the line at styling my hair. That was probably for the best anyway. In the beginning the most difficult part was getting a haircut right before I was in the wheelchair. My legs weren't strong enough to lift my body into the salon chair. We just did the best we could but often I was not seated properly. The salon that I used was not accessible to a power wheelchair. I knew I had to find a fully accessible salon and a stylist that would be comfortable learning to operate my wheelchair in the future. I had been lucky enough to find Shelly before I was in the wheelchair. When I no longer had the strength to use nail clippers I went to her for pedicures. We got to know each other and I knew she would take good care of my hair and the salon was perfect for my wheelchair. Shelly has a great sense of humor that is not unlike my own. While I was still walking independently, I was sitting in the salon chair getting a haircut. When an older man came in, using a cane, I said, "Look Shelly, that is me someday." Without missing a beat Shelly said, "Oh girl, you passed him a long time ago." We both laughed. Shelly works part time as a stylist and works as a waitress when she isn't at the salon. She is so sweet. Now that I can't get into the pedicure chair she comes to my house and takes care of my feet.

Then I decided to have my hair washed and styled weekly. Since Shelly's schedule was less flexible I needed a new person and was lucky enough to find Caitlin. At first I could position the wheelchair and change positions as needed. Now I can drive to the shampoo area, turn around and back my chair up to the shampoo bowl. After that Caitlin takes over. She is so good with my chair and, even though my speech is almost unintelligible, she still understands sometimes.

Hair, make-up, jewelry, and wardrobe are such a part of one's identity and gender. They reflect who and where you are. When you have ALS you lose who you were bit by bit and become a new version of yourself.

This chapter lets you in on the barriers faced by folks in power wheelchairs. Keep in mind that it isn't just one barrier to a building it is a landscape of barriers for people in power wheelchairs, not to a building but to people, celebrations and ceremonies. It is not feasible to think that there could be a world fully accessible to power wheelchairs. It would be wonderful if, as a people, we could commit to making progress toward inclusion in public places. Until then try garage sitting, at least.

CHAPTER 7

Exquisite Bittersweet Joy

When Ed and I got married in 1978 he came with a special bonus, a five year old daughter. Tracy had beautiful long golden hair that curled ever so slightly on the bottom. She loved playing outside, walking on her tiptoes and doing anything with her daddy. We had good times together but she had the unfortunate task of teaching me how to be a mom. People often say that your first child is your practice child and your subsequent children benefit from lessons learned. When that first child is a stepchild and she is already five years old it can be likened to hitting the ground running. There were many 'firsts' with her and she was a good teacher.

As time went on our family grew as we were blessed to have a daughter, Charity, and a son, Wes. When they were growing up I vowed not to be a parent who would look back with regret for not spending time with their children. I was fortunate enough to work within schools so that when they were home I was home. Even our birthdays were close. Charity, was born October 7th and two years later Wes, was born on October 5th. My birthday? October 6th. We didn't celebrate a birthday at our house, we had birthday week. I feel blessed to have authentic, genuine relationships with them as adults. I couldn't be prouder of them.

In October of 2010 Charity came to celebrate birthdays. She presented me with the best gift ever, a sonogram picture. She and David were going to have my first grandchild, a girl.

With ALS no matter what kind of day you're having, tomorrow will be worse. Looking into the future was something I made a practice of avoiding. I wondered, would I still be here when it was time for her to be born? I was simultaneously ecstatic and heartsick. Privately I grieved. This was a big deal and I told myself I had the right to grieve.

I would not get to watch her grow up.

I would not get to be the gramma that I wanted to be.

I would not hold her, sing to her or read to her.

There would be no tea parties or helping her make cookies.

There would be no walks to the park or playing with dolls.

I could have stayed in the darkness, but I once again decided, "Not today." Giving up would have been easy, but how could I? Today was all I had. As long as it was in my power I did not want to miss any of the joy of this pregnancy. I wanted to hear all about the doctor visits, and I did. Charity called after each appointment and kept me updated on how she felt. I would have missed so much if I had given up. I was able to be with her during labor and meet my granddaughter before she was two hours old, our beautiful Becca.

I was able to spend time with them throughout the first week at home. The nursery doorway was too small to accommodate the 'companion' chair I was using but I could see it all. As any other grandmother I wanted to get something special for the room so we went shopping. In the Chicago area we were able to go to both Babies R Us and Buy Buy Baby, neither of which we had in our town. We bought a lamp that matched the nursery linens, a stuffed bear that played music and a lullaby CD. What fun!

A couple of weeks later my daughter and granddaughter came and spent a week at our house. I can't think of anything more generous. When my children were born I am not sure I could have been so generous. It was equally generous on the part of my son-in-law. David was so awesome as a new dad and I know it was quite difficult for him to share his new baby girl and his wife with me.

At the time of this writing we are preparing to celebrate her first birthday! How cool is that!?!

CHAPTER 8

Seriously, I'm Not Making This Up

I worked my entire life in the field of disability services. So, I was not surprised at some of the things that happened to me.

After I was in the wheelchair people would, without regard, lean on my chair. Friends, family members, casual acquaintances and perfect strangers leaned on different parts of my chair. Sometimes they weren't even talking to me. My comfort level was usually proportionate to the level of familiarity with the individual. The only people who can lean on it, whether they are talking to me or not, is my immediate family or really close friends. I don't like strangers doing it at all. I hate it when anyone bumps my chair; I've always been that way - even a regular chair or my bed. Who knows where that came from?

For a great deal of my life I was a sign language interpreter for deaf people. How weird that at this stage I need someone to interpret for me. It was part of my identity and a great source of pride and satisfaction to me. Thanks to ALS I had the distinct experience of losing my voice twice. With sign language I could watch the loss happen. With voice my mind played tricks on me. When I started to become less articulate I judged how understandable I was by other people and not what I heard in my head. Now that my speech is really bad I don't expect to be understood. Recently my voice was inadvertently recorded in the background of a family gathering and when I heard it I cried and immediately tried to say, "Shut it off, shut it off". Of course I was not understood so I turned my chair around and left the room. I immediately 'flashed' on the times we were in stores and I spoke to Ed and strangers turned to find the source of the voice. That being said, I still try to talk to close family and friends. Sometimes I get frustrated but many times it can be really funny and we both end up laughing. One time Ed was getting me ready for the day and I was trying to tell him that the slacks in his hands had a tear in the "crotch". Ed kept repeating, "You want something from the garage?" "You want me to put them in the garage?" "You want to go to the garage?" While this was a terrible contextual guess, it wasn't a bad speech reading guess. Try saying those two words and see how they feel in your mouth. Anyway, I started to laugh and when I laughed my speech just got worse. At this point Ed didn't yet know why it was so funny but the harder I laughed the more he laughed. It can be pretty ridiculous.

Don't fake understanding. It can be insulting. Now, my voice is a slightly improved female version of Steven Hawking. I could have 'banked' my voice before I lost it. Professionals would have used a specific computer software program to record my voice so it could be used to program the text to speech program for my current computer. That way when I 'tell' my computer to speak for me it would 'speak' with my voice. I chose not to do that for a couple of reasons. I thought it might be unnerving to hear a mechanical version of my own voice and I never really liked the sound of my voice anyway.

Once I was clearly becoming less articulate people often yelled at me. Some people spoke to me in the ways they thought they should speak to a child or a person with an intellectual disability. By the way, if you are speaking to a person with an intellectual disability in a funny voice you are embarrassing yourself.

Other things that happened to me were more of a surprise. Some really caught me off guard. They made me wonder about the civility of our society. Were these people ignorant, self-absorbed, thoughtless, well intentioned or just plain mean? I'll let you decide.

While I was still walking independently without too much difficulty I was trying out different salons and hair dressers. On my first meeting with one stylist, as she was styling my hair, she said, "You might be interested to know that I also go to the funeral homes and do hair." REALLY!?! What could I do at that point? My hair was still wet.

Shortly after diagnosis a woman brought me a funeral planning guide. Enough said.

I was in the wheelchair, no longer able to feed myself but my speech was still easily understood. We went to Panera Bread which, as you probably know, serves lunch and has a bakery counter. After we finished eating we stopped to buy some bakery items to take home. Translation - Ed was busy and I had parked off to the side. A middle aged woman walked directly up to me and inquired, "Do you mind if I ask why you are in the wheelchair?" Okay, polite and respectful. She asked if I had experienced a stroke. I really didn't mind and if I had minded she left me an 'out'. I thought it gave me an opportunity to expand awareness and understanding of ALS. I told her I had ALS and asked if she knew what that was. Exactly what does an individual like her plan as a follow up comment? Here is where it got weird for me. As if I just turned purple and sprouted orange horns she said, "But, you're smiling…" It took a fair amount of self-control to not respond, "Would you prefer I cry?" Her response?? "Your smile is a gift to others every day." While some people might find that kind and sweet it gave me the creeps. I was not trying to be a martyr. I was smiling because I felt like it.

While I was in pretty much the same shape as the previous story we went to Cracker Barrel for dinner. As you know, they have a large area with display after display of merchandise for sale. We had a brief wait so I was trying to navigate through the narrow paths around the displays. A middle aged woman approached me and said, "It is so good to see you out!" For a minute I thought, 'Do I know this woman?' Then she said, "I love your hair." This couldn't be a case of mistaken identity. How many women in power wheelchairs could she possibly know? Then it just kept getting weirder. "You are beautiful." Now she was grasping at straws for something to keep this conversation going. I had to roll my eyes at that one. She saw my response and added, "No, really, you are beautiful." I had to roll away as I shook my head. Who does something like that to a complete stranger? Would she have said those things if I hadn't been in my wheelchair? I don't think so.

About a year after diagnosis a friend stopped by for a visit. At this time, of course, I did not look like anything was wrong with me. Although this person knew of my diagnosis I truly believe they had a temporary lapse of memory. They were really frustrated from dealing with an aging family member who was experiencing a significant decline in functioning. Thousands of people have probably uttered a similar phrase. It has many variations on a theme. "If I ever get like that just hit me in the head with a cast iron skillet." To this day I don't know if they realized what they said.

Riding sideways is a challenge and one that cannot be faced alone. Still, I have planned for the future. I continue to live for today. I am thankful for a million things, most importantly my husband, Ed. If there are crowns given out in heaven for selflessness then he should receive a lavish one. I laugh . . . a lot . . . every day. I have ALS. It doesn't have me, not today.

Made in the USA
Lexington, KY
27 January 2013